W9-BEL-175

COLONIAL PEOPLE

The Tanner

CHRISTINE PETERSEN

 **Marshall Cavendish**
Benchmark
New York

Published by Marshall Cavendish Benchmark
An imprint of Marshall Cavendish Corporation

Other Marshall Cavendish Offices:

Marshall Cavendish International (Asia) Private Limited, 1 New Industrial Road, Singapore 536196 • Marshall Cavendish
International (Thailand) Co Ltd., 253 Asoke, 12th Flr, Sukhumvit 21 Road, Klongtoey Nua, Wattana, Bangkok 10110,
Thailand • Marshall Cavendish (Malaysia) Sdn Bhd, Times Subang, Lot 46, Subang Hi-Tech Industrial Park, Batu Tiga,
40000 Shah Alam, Selangor Darul Ehsan, Malaysia

Marshall Cavendish is a trademark of Times Publishing Limited

All websites were available and accurate when this book was sent to press.

Library of Congress Cataloging-in-Publication Data

Petersen, Christine.
The tanner / Christine Petersen.
p. cm. — (Colonial people)
Includes index.
Summary: "Explore the life of a colonial tanner and his importance to the
community, as well as everyday life, responsibilities, and social practices
during that time"—Provided by publisher.
ISBN 978-1-60870-418-7 (Print); 978-1-60870-640-2 (eBook)
1. Tanners—United States—History—17th century—Juvenile literature.
2. Tanners—United States—History—18th century—Juvenile literature.
3. Leather industry and trade—United States—History—17th century—Juvenile
literature. 4. Leather industry and trade—United States—History—18th
century—Juvenile literature. 5. United States—History—Colonial period,
ca. 1600–1775—Juvenile literature. I. Title.
TS965.5.P48 2012
675'.239097309033—dc22
2010033896

Editor: Joy Bean
Publisher: Michelle Bisson
Art Director: Anahid Hamparian
Series Designer: Kay Petronio

Expert Reader: Paul Douglas Newman, Ph.D., Department of History, University of Pittsburgh at Johnstown

Photo research by Marybeth Kavanagh

Printed in Malaysia (T)
135642

CONTENTS

ONE

Hopes and Hardships

English colonists came to America in 1607 with their heads filled with dreams. They had heard remarkable stories about Virginia, a stretch of land along the Atlantic coastline of North America. England had claimed this land two decades earlier, when early English explorers found forests lush with trees and fur-bearing animals. Most of England's own woodlands had been cleared to provide firewood and space for farms and fields. By the early seventeenth century, many citizens of England had crowded into cities to seek jobs that were not available in the countryside.

Woodlands were not the only temptation in Virginia. Fishermen who sailed the nearby seas came back with ship holds overflowing with fish. Even more exciting were the rumors about Spanish ships filled with gold from the New World. If the colonists found riches

Colonists unload supplies shipped from England for their settlement in colonial Virginia.

like these, they could ship the goods back to England and make a huge profit.

The idea of quick riches was tempting for working-class Englishmen, who left conditions of poverty and overcrowding. About half the first colonists were gentlemen—a class of men born into wealthy and powerful families. But most of the gentlemen colonists were younger sons who were not first in line to inherit land. Like the working-class settlers, the gentlemen expected to spend a short time in Virginia and return home wealthy enough to buy their own land and to improve their positions in English society.

Jamestown Survivors

These first colonists didn't know what challenges they would face in Virginia. It was a lonely life, far from familiar people and places. While establishing their settlement at Jamestown, many men suffered from injuries and serious illnesses. But hunger was the biggest problem. None of the men were farmers, and most of them refused to do hard physical labor. Instead of planting crops, the men relied on corn purchased from American Indians, or they stored the food they had brought from home as they hunted for treasure.

In 1608, the hungry Jamestown settlers were fortunate when two supply ships arrived with new colonists and more food. That same year, however, fire destroyed all of the colonists' houses,

The Promised Land

The British government gave any man who paid his own passage to Virginia a piece of land to farm, as well as additional land for each family member or servant he brought along. The government established similar programs as other colonies formed. Soon the Virginians used a system of indentured servitude, in which wealthy colonists paid for other settlers to travel from England to the new world. Poor people could choose to become indentured servants, but most were criminals or wards of the government, forced to leave jails and poorhouses for North America. This practice helped ease overcrowding in England's prisons.

Indentured servants, including those who worked as tanners, were told that they would receive land in America, along with the tools they needed to farm it. This should have been a promising situation, for no poor Englishman could have hoped to own land at home. But there was a catch. First the servants had to pay back the colonist who had sponsored their voyage. Servants paid in years of service. Many worked on farms, although some received training in a craft, such as tanning. It was a hard life. Indentured servants were worked to the bone, and only a small percentage survived their years of service to collect the land they had been promised in Virginia.

and rats ate much of their stored grain. The men finally planted corn in spring 1609, but their crops grew poorly.

In some uneasy trades with the local Powhatan Indian tribes, the colonists exchanged metal tools for corn and meat. This arrangement stopped in the spring of 1609, when seven ships brought several hundred men and women from England. Powhatan leaders knew what the colonists' increasing population meant—the settlers would soon spread across the countryside,

Jamestown colony's small fort was beside the James River.

taking more land for themselves. Hoping to drive the colonists away, the Powhatan stopped providing food and began regular attacks on Jamestown.

The colonists spent the winter of 1609 inside their small, triangular town. Its wooden walls protected them from Indian attacks, but they were unable to hunt or to gather food to supplement the small amount of corn they had grown. The people were so desperate for food that they ate shoes or any other source of **leather** they could find.

When two English supply ships arrived at Jamestown in spring 1610, only sixty survivors remained. The exhausted colonists were ready to go home to England. On June 7 they packed up and boarded the ships. George Percy, who was president of Jamestown, described what happened next: "[All] of us [were] sailing down the river with a full intent to have proceeded upon our voyage for England, when suddenly we espied a boat making towards us. . . ." The English government had sent a new leader to the colony. He had food, weapons, and a new batch of colonists— including the first group of tanners.

TWO

Honest and Industrious Men

Jamestown colonists welcomed the arrival of tanners. These **craftsmen** were skilled at making leather from animal skins and hides. Leather was one of the most useful materials available in the seventeenth century. People used it to make everything from saddles and suitcases to drinking mugs and drum covers. The most important use for leather, however, was to make shoes.

Colonists were told to bring several pairs of boots when they sailed to Jamestown. But because the men walked everywhere, and were outside in all kinds of weather, their footwear quickly wore out. Supply ships from England came so infrequently that colonists could not easily replace broken boots and shoes. Splits, cracks, and tears in the leather were serious health risks. A simple blister might cause infection, which could be deadly in the 1600s. Shoemakers arrived along with the tanners in 1610. These two groups of craftsmen worked together to provide a good supply of footwear in Jamestown.

By now, the Jamestown colonists had figured out that they were unlikely to find gold or other easy riches in Virginia. The key to their success was to profit from the land by farming, cutting timber, and collecting animal skins. In 1611 the colonists began to advertise in England and Europe. They called for "honest and industrious men . . . and laboring men of all sorts" to join the colony. In particular, the company sought more tanners, shoemakers, and other craftsmen. The colonial leaders offered gifts to each colonist who paid a fare to Virginia. "[He] shall be furnished with necessary tooles of all sorts," they offered, "and for his better subsistence he shall have Poultry, and swine, and if he deserve it, a Goate or two, perhaps a cow given him."

Two fleets of ships, bearing six hundred men, arrived in Jamestown in

Advertisements like this tried to make life in the colonies seem exciting and profitable.

Cattle Come to the Colonies

Every seventeenth-century European community raised cattle and other livestock for food and leather. But the British were not the first Europeans to bring these animals to the New World. The Spanish took cattle along when they began to colonize Mexico and the Caribbean islands in the early

sixteenth century. Settlers raised cattle in Spain's colony of Florida, on the Atlantic coastline south of Virginia. The French established the colony of Quebec in 1608, and within a dozen years had imported cattle from France. As in Jamestown, leaders of the Dutch colonies used cattle and other livestock to reward colonists who journeyed to New Netherlands. Beginning in 1625, Dutch settlers received cows, sheep, pigs, and horses when they moved to the island of *Manhatas* (now known as Manhattan).

Livestock were eventually shipped to Jamestown, providing leather for that colony's tanners. And in 1620 England's second major colony was founded hundreds of miles north of Virginia, at Plymouth, Massachusetts. Its settlers were members of the Congregationalist Church, sometimes known as Pilgrims or Puritans. In 1624, a ship brought the first four cows to Plymouth. Livestock soon became common in all colonial communities.

1611. The colonists had received chickens, pigs, and sheep in 1608. A few of the colony's gentlemen may even have sent for horses from England. But these were the first cows the Virginians had seen since leaving England. It was a high priority to protect the stock from bad weather and attacks by predators or American Indians. The colonists built a stable and waited for the herd to grow before eating any of the precious beasts.

Thomas West, Lord De La Warr, had supervised the expedition that brought colonists and livestock to Jamestown in 1610. When he returned to England in spring 1611, De La Warr reported that "the cattell [cattle] already there are much encreased [increased] and thrive exceedingly well with the pasture of that Country." The residents of Jamestown were grateful for this familiar addition to their environment. Cows provided milk that people could use to make many nutritious and filling foods, such as buttermilk, butter, and cheese. Male cattle, called **steers**, were raised for beef.

The tanner received a steer's remains after farmers or butchers collected the meat. Because the steers' thick hide was the best source of leather, it was often as valuable as the meat itself. A cow's hooves were also useful. When boiled, they released a type of oil that the tanner used to soften leather. The tanner received other types of livestock skins as well. Although goat, sheep, and pig leather were not as thick and durable as steer leather, colonists liked the softness and flexibility of leather from these other animals.

With the addition of hardworking colonists and a military program to fight the American Indians, the colony of Jamestown finally began to grow. Carpenters, shoemakers, tailors, and tanners worked alongside laborers, servants, farmers, and colonial leaders. Instead of attacking the settlers, American Indians became eager to trade animal skins with the colonists. The tanners used the additional leather from native peoples to meet the needs of several hundred colonists.

The leaders of Jamestown also began to buy land from the Powhatan. They paid the American Indians in small amounts of corn. As the Powhatan had feared, the English colonists were planning to stay.

Tanners worked on the skins of goats, sheep, and pigs, as well as cattle.

THREE

Made of Leather

Colonial Americans used a wide variety of goods in their daily lives. They ate food prepared in cookware, wore clothing, worked with tools, and rode in animal-powered vehicles. Seventeenth-century colonists generally lived in small villages or on isolated farms. Buying, repairing, or replacing goods could be challenging. Farmers went to town when they could. They took advantage of the chance to **barter** with neighbors by providing a product or service in return for something they needed.

If a village had a general store, it sold a variety of products imported from England, Europe, or the Caribbean islands. Owners of the village general store paid attention to the needs of their local customers and stocked a variety of goods. Along with food items, shoppers might find medicines and even simple articles of clothing. A colonist who needed a new pair of shoes probably had to get them from England, however. Colonists delivered their orders to the nearest port town, to be sent with the next ship. The English shoemaker obtained leather from a tanner and made the shoes, which he then shipped back to the colonies. If the shoes made it that far undamaged by seawater or ship rats, they were combined with other orders, packed on a cart, and pulled by horse or oxen along bumpy, muddy colonial roads to their destination. In all, it might take a year for a colonist to receive those new shoes.

The long wait for essential goods inspired many colonists to become more independent. They learned to make or mend the goods they required for daily survival. A practical farmer learned to build a fire appropriate for heating iron so that he could fix broken tools. He grew crops such as flax or raised sheep, and his wife could use either product to spin thread that was woven into material for clothing. A farmer skilled in woodworking could make furniture and build or repair his house. Some farmers also found it useful to **tan** their own leather. Those who were able to tolerate this time-consuming and smelly process could make leather for their own use. Leather was a valuable product to barter with neighbors.

The colonial general store, as reenacted in Colonial Williamsburg, offered items the colonists could not make at home. Some leather goods were shipped from England and sold in the store.

The Tanner Comes to Town

Colonial farmers got by with homemade leather, but it was rarely their first choice. It was rough against their skin, it tended to crack, and therefore did not last as long as the fine leather made by experts. It was a relief for colonists when skilled tanners arrived to take over the work. By the eighteenth century most villages had a tanner, and townspeople could always locate a **tanyard** factory by following its smell. Colonists generally preferred to build the tanyard on the edge of town, in a place where winds would not carry the odor of skins and tanning chemicals toward houses and other buildings. This request may have seemed like an insult, but the tanner knew it was simply practical. The tanner was highly respected in his community because he provided a product that people could not live without.

So Many Uses

Even though tanners had arrived in North America, many colonists continued to buy leather goods, such as saddles and shoe soles, from England. Shoe soles, which were made of exceptionally thick leather, were difficult to produce, and it took colonial tanners a long time to get the process right.

Only a small percentage of colonists owned horses. Most settlers preferred oxen or cattle, which did not carry humans but

The Fur Trade

While much of the leather made by colonial tanners came from livestock, a significant portion was produced from wild animals. Deer, elk, and bison skins made good leather that was preferred by some buyers. Hunters and trappers sometimes

ventured into the wilderness to catch animals, but it was very common to trade with American Indians. Tribes that lived in the woodlands and mountains had access to large populations of wild animals. They set up a barter system with colonial traders and their French competitors. Traders offered goods that were valuable to American Indians. Warm woolen blankets, cooking pans, metal weapons, and glass or porcelain beads were among the settlers' most popular offerings.

Many colonists wore beaver hats, and these also became popular in Europe. But the tanner had plenty of work, so a different group of craftsmen prepared furs. Women often did the first step of removing the fur from a beaver skin. Other craftsmen pressed the fur together, making a warm and waterproof fabric called felt that could be shaped into hats. Hat making became an industry in Connecticut, Rhode Island, and elsewhere. In 1720, approximately 6 percent of the money that English merchants paid to colonial Americans was for the purchase of animal skins and furs.

were well suited to doing work on the farm. People who lived in town did not need horses, for everything they needed was within walking distance. Because the demand for saddles was so low, few tanners bothered to make them. But tanners did meet the colonists'

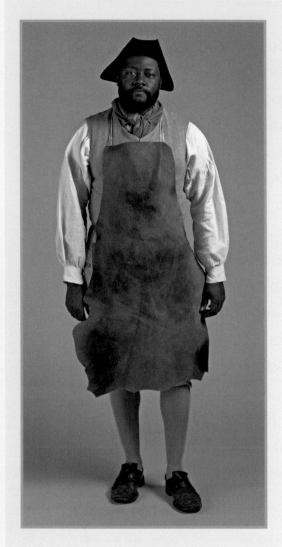

A craftsman in his leather apron, as reenacted in Colonial Williamsburg.

many other needs for leather, and tanning developed into an important colonial industry.

Leather was an irreplaceable material used to make a wide range of everyday goods. In addition to boots and shoes, colonial people wore many leather articles of clothing. Some breeches, or knee-length pants, were made of leather so that colonists would have a layer of protection while working outdoors. The short doublet vest or jacket that a man wore over his shirt could also be made of leather. Craftsmen wore leather aprons over their clothing. Hunters or explorers might choose to wear an entire outfit made of deerskin, which was also called buckskin. This material provided warmth and camouflage for people who lived outdoors for long periods of time. Soldiers were sometimes assigned to patrol the edges of colonial territory, where they might fight American Indians or colonists from other European countries. They wore leather armor. The material was not as strong as metal, but it was much lighter and not as hot.

Although the tanner did not make many saddles, people often asked him to produce harnesses. These straps connected a horse, cow, or ox to a cart. Carts and other vehicles also contained parts made of leather. Before metal springs were invented, people used strips of leather to attach a vehicle's body to its wheels. More elaborate vehicles, such as carriages, had leather-covered seats, curtains, and hoods.

Settlers also used the tanner's leather to cover luggage and a variety of other containers. Cavalrymen filled leather saddlebags with their belongings and slung them over their horses' backs. Soldiers used leather-covered boxes to protect their guns and ammunition. On their backs they carried swords and muskets tucked into leather cases.

Many colonial household items were made of leather. Wealthy settlers chose this material to cover their books, and they wrote on thin sheets of leather called **vellum**.

Some colonists drank from blackjacks, which were mugs made of leather and lined with tree sap to keep them from leaking.

With such a high demand for leather, the tanner was always busy.

A leather drinking mug, or blackjack.

FOUR

In the Tanyard

A boy rarely chose his career in colonial America. The eldest son of a craftsman usually followed in his father's footsteps. He became an **apprentice** and studied with a master craftsman. The master might accept other boys from the community as apprentices as well. Apprentices were not paid, but they were expected to work from sunrise to sunset six days a week. Just as a father could punish his son for misbehavior, a master was within his rights to discipline an apprentice. Over a period of years the master passed along all of his knowledge and skills—the "art and mystery" of his craft. If the boy worked hard, his education was complete by the age of twenty-one. He received a set of tools from the master and became a **journeyman**. The journeyman might remain in the same tanyard as a paid employee, but he was also free to seek work in another village, a city, or a large plantation.

Cleaning Up

The tanner taught his apprentice to make many different types of leather. Most of the skins that the tanyard received were from cattle, as most colonists liked beef. Ox, calf, sheep, pig, and goat skins were also common. On occasion the tanner received a more unusual item—bear, shark or ray, snake or lizard, or even dolphin.

The tanner bought some skins from the butcher. These were ideal, for they were usually fresh, and the tanner was able to sell all of the leather he made. Most other skins came from farmers who butchered animals at home. A farmer did not sell his skins to the tanner; he needed the leather. Instead, they made a deal. In exchange for his services, the tanner would keep a portion of the leather. The farmer wanted to be sure he received his own leather rather than another farmer's, as someone else's leather might be of poorer quality. The tanner guaranteed this by marking every skin when it arrived. He did the same for hunters who delivered wild animal skins.

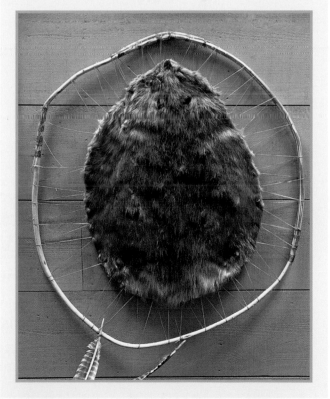

Animal skins were stretched to help them dry.

Dyeing Fabric

Tannins give color to animal skins and preserve them from natural processes of decay. Fabric can also be dyed. Although this process is not identical to tanning, it gives a sense of the time-consuming work colonists undertook to produce materials we use every day.

You Will Need

- a small, clean piece of white or natural-colored cotton fabric
- water
- vinegar
- red cabbage or spinach
- a measuring cup
- a cooking pot
- a wire strainer
- a large bowl
- a wooden spoon
- metal tongs
- potholders
- a cloth or plastic apron
- rubber or vinyl gloves

Instructions

1. Put on an apron.

2. Ask an adult to help you in the kitchen. Put two cups (0.5 l) of water and one-half cup (125 ml) of vinegar in the cooking pot. Place on stove and bring to a boil over medium heat.

3. Carefully place the piece of fabric in the pot. Reduce the heat and simmer for one hour. Check frequently and use the spoon to push the fabric down if it is not fully immersed in water.

4. After an hour, turn off the stove. Have an adult carry the pot to the sink. Use potholders! Use the tongs to move the fabric carefully from the pan into the sink.

5. Run the cloth under cold water for about a minute. Squeeze extra water from the cloth, and leave it in the sink.

6. Wash and dry your cooking pot. Be cautious in case it is still hot.

7. Decide which plant material you want to use. Red cabbage turns the fabric pale purple or blue. Spinach makes the fabric green. Cut the plant material into small pieces. You need enough to fill one cup (0.25 l). Dump the chopped plant pieces into the cooking pan.

8. Add two cups (0.5 l) of water and bring to a boil. Reduce the heat and allow the mixture to simmer for one hour. Check the pot frequently.

9. With an adult, pour the water slowly through a wire strainer into a large bowl. You can compost or throw away the leftover plant material.

10. Add your fabric to the colored water. Stir to soak every part of the fabric. The longer you soak the cloth, the darker the color will be. You can leave it overnight, but be sure to stir it once or twice to keep the color even.

11. Be sure to wear the apron and gloves to avoid stains, and use tongs when you remove the fabric from the bowl. Rinse the fabric in cold water again, and squeeze out excess liquid. Allow it to dry, and your fabric should retain its color. Wash it by hand rather than with other items in the washing machine.

12. Cut off a small corner of your fabric and examine it from the side. You'll notice that the color has soaked through from top to bottom. Colonial tanners did the same thing to make sure tannins had reached every part of a thick skin. If the skin absorbed the tannins unevenly, the leather would begin to rot.

If a farmer or hunter was unable to visit the tanner immediately after killing an animal, he preserved the skin by rubbing salt on its surface. This caused the skin to dry stiffly and could prevent it from rotting for months. The tanner's first step was to trim the skin's rough edges, which would not make good leather.

Next, the tanner had to remove the salt. He started by alternately rinsing and scrubbing the skin. During this process the skin began to soften and to become more flexible. The tanner then dipped the skin in a vat containing **lime** and water. Lime was made from seashells that had been crushed and melted. It contained high levels of calcium, a chemical that seeped into the skin and loosened the hairs. Depending on the size of the skin, it might take weeks for lime to do its job.

The tanner knew when the liming process was complete because hairs began to fall off when he touched the skin. At this point he pulled the skin from the vat, let it drain, and stretched it over a rounded wooden beam. Although the hairs were loose, it was still hard work to clean them from the skin. For this job the tanner used a long, dull knife with a handle at each end. The beam was usually tipped downward, which provided a good angle for the tanner to scrape the knife back and forth over the skin. Periodically he used water to flush loose hair onto the ground.

The tanner might have to soak a skin in the lime solution and scrape it several times before all the hair came off. When this was done, he repeated the process to clean off any flesh that clung to the underside of the skin.

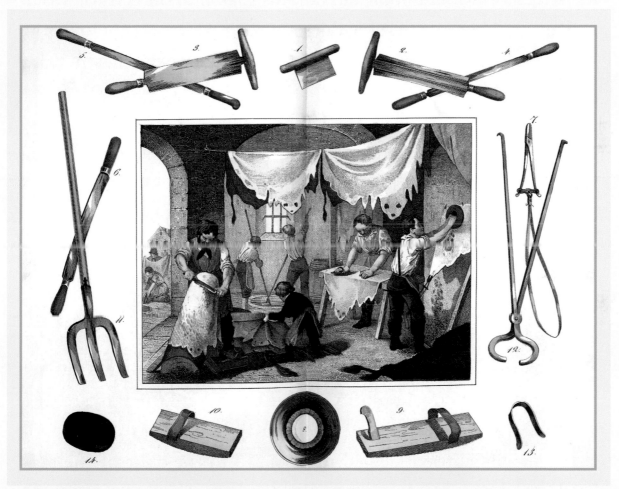

The tanner needed many different tools to do his work, from tongs and pitchforks to knives and grindstones.

The Cure

Once a skin was clean, the tanner had to **cure** it. The key to this process was tannin, a yellowish-brown chemical found in tree bark. Animal skins absorb the color of tannin, which gives leather its rich color. More important, tannins soak into the cells of a skin and harden them, so the skin does not rot. Oak trees contained the strongest tannins. Tanners could also use hemlock, chestnut, fir, and sumac bark.

The tanbark mill was designed to grind tree bark into small bits. It was a simple but efficient machine. First, the builder set a tall post into the ground. Then he attached a second, horizontal beam to the post. He harnessed an ox or other large animal to the far end of the beam. In the middle of the beam stood a wide stone wheel. The animal pushed the wheel as it walked around the center post. The rough surface of the heavy wheel crushed any bark placed in its path. People collected the tannin powder and formed it into cubes that were easy to transport. A tanner might set up his own tanbark mill if he had a large tanyard and access to a good supply of appropriate trees.

A tanner's apprentice had to get used to the odor of the tanyard, which was unlike any smell he had encountered previously. The pungent chemical vapors filled the air and eventually seeped

Don't Drink the Water

Because every step of the tanning process required freshwater, it was practical for tanners to build their yards near streams. This practice had negative consequences, however. The tanner not only took water from the stream, but also released a lot of waste into it. Large amounts of salt, lime, and tannins flowed downstream from every tanyard. Another common pollutant was a mixture of animal dung, salt, and water called bate. This substance helped tanners remove lime and soften skins.

Tanyards were not the only sources of water pollution in colonial times. Gristmills and sawmills were also located alongside streams, sometimes near the tanyards. Gristmills ground wheat, corn, and other grains to produce flour, while sawmills cut trees into boards for construction. Mill workers dumped flour and sawdust into nearby streams. Worse yet, other colonists regularly dumped trash, animal carcasses, and sewage into local water sources.

Colonists did not always realize that their actions polluted the water—but they did know that the water was rarely safe to drink. They usually chose drinks with a low alcohol content, such as ale, cider, or wine. These drinks had a different set of health risks, but the alcohol may have killed some of the disease-causing organisms to which colonists were exposed.

Tree bark was ground in a large mill to obtain tannins for curing leather.

into his hair and clothing. At first his eyes watered from the strong vapors. He was likely a little scared to see his skin pucker in places where the liquid tannin splattered onto it. It was part of the apprentice's training to ignore these side effects and to carry on with his work.

Curing took place in square or rectangular pits in the ground. Tanyards usually had a series of side-by-side pits filled with water. The tanner laid his skins in the water with a small amount of crushed tanbark between them. The name for this tea-colored, stinking mixture was **ooze**. Apprentices walked between the pits and used long sticks to turn the skins. Sometimes they lifted the heavy, waterlogged skins completely out of the ooze to drain and then returned them to the pits to soak some more. The tanner continually added more tanbark until the ooze reached a perfect balance of tannin and water.

It might take a year or more for the tannins to seep into every part of a skin. The tanner checked the skins by cutting off corners now and then. When the inside of the skin had an even color, it was ready to come out of the tanning pits. The tanner rinsed the skin in a stream until no excess tannins ran off. Then he hung the skin over a pole in his shed, which had a roof but no walls. The dried skin had turned into hard, dark leather.

Though tough and durable at this stage, the leather was still too rough to use for anything other than making shoe soles. Another process called **currying** made leather soft and smooth. Some tanners curried their own leather, but a separate craftsman usually did this work. A currier used many techniques to finish the

leather. After soaking it in water, he might beat or stretch it. Oils rubbed into the leather's surface made it bendable. The finished product was ready for use by craftsmen such as shoemakers or tailors—and it was far more comfortable for colonists to wear.

The tanner hung a cured skin on a beam to scrape off the hairs.

FIVE

The Law of the Land

England's leaders were mostly happy about the growth of the American colonies. The English government saw colonial America as a source of income. The British wanted the colonists to provide much-needed raw materials and, at the same time, to purchase goods made in England. Colonists disagreed with this thinking. Over the decades, they made more products for themselves, and they were eager to buy and sell goods wherever business was best.

In the mid-seventeenth century, in order to get colonists to buy goods from their mother country, England passed the Navigation Acts. These laws required that goods from the colonies be transported in either English or colonial ships. This meant the colonists could not sell their goods to Dutch merchants, who were their neighbors in America. A 1660 amendment to the Navigation Acts stated that certain valuable goods produced in the colonies could be shipped only to England or its other colonies. The goods were taxed when they arrived in England or when they were sold from one colony to another. Tobacco, rice, skins, and furs were on this list of valuable goods.

Colonists became frustrated with these laws and ignored them when possible. But England was an important market. Britain's demand for skins and furs was so great that colonists began to travel farther west in search of new locations to hunt and to trade. The colonists came into conflict with French traders on the western boundary of England's territory. In 1756, the French and Indian War began. England and France fought for possession of the Ohio Valley. American Indians in this area initially supported the French, who had been their allies for several years. After seven years, however, the French finally surrendered their sprawling territory, which stretched from the Appalachian Mountains west to the Mississippi River.

Colonists were happy to move into their new land. But the English government had a surprise in store. The British

After the Navigation Acts were passed, colonists could only ship their goods to England or its settlements.

The Other Workers

In the 1750s, Virginia's capital, Williamsburg, was a bustling center of colonial trade. William Pearson's tanyard was one of several in the town. His setup exemplified the complexity and size that tanning operations could achieve. Pearson owned tan vats, bark houses, a mill house, and a fleshing house, where new skins were taken to be cleaned before being cured. He certainly would have had apprentices, but Pearson also kept slaves.

Slavery was very common in colonial America, especially in the southern colonies. Craftsmen sometimes found it frustrating to train one apprentice after another and then watch each one leave. For some, the logical solution was to purchase slaves. The way a colonist saw it, slaves were an investment. Like indentured servants, slaves were expensive. But unlike other kinds of workers, slaves never left. In his tanyard Pearson had seven slaves, four of whom were trained in the craft.

Approximately 250,000 slaves were brought to the colonies during the eighteenth century. Most came from the west coast of Africa. Although people throughout the English colonies had slaves, they were most common in the southern colonies, whose large tobacco and rice farms required many hands to function.

In Maryland and Virginia, slaves made up 40 percent of the population. Enslaved Africans developed communities enriched by music, new languages, and religions that meshed African spirituality with Christianity. But in all cases, slaves were always at the mercy of an owner—they were property that could be mistreated or sent away on a whim.

predicted that American Indians would be angry to see the French go. To calm the Indian tribes, the English established a boundary. Settlers were to remain on the east side, and American Indian tribes were to stay on the west. Government officials hoped that in a few years they would be able to establish a friendly relationship with American Indian tribes. This would make it safe for colonists to move in, and it would guarantee that skins and furs would continue to flow to England. Colonists mostly ignored this boundary, just as they had ignored the Navigation Acts. At the same time, however, many colonists began to desire independence from England and its laws. They wanted free access to American Indian land.

In 1767, colonists faced a new law. England was deeply in debt from the French and Indian War. Parliament passed a new law that funneled money to the British government by taxing many items imported to the colonies from England. Among those items were leather saddles and shoe soles. The effect was powerful. Many colonists began to **boycott** English goods. Local craftsmen worked hard to provide the same products at more reasonable prices.

In 1776, a group of patriots met in Philadelphia to declare the thirteen colonies' independence from England. Their statement

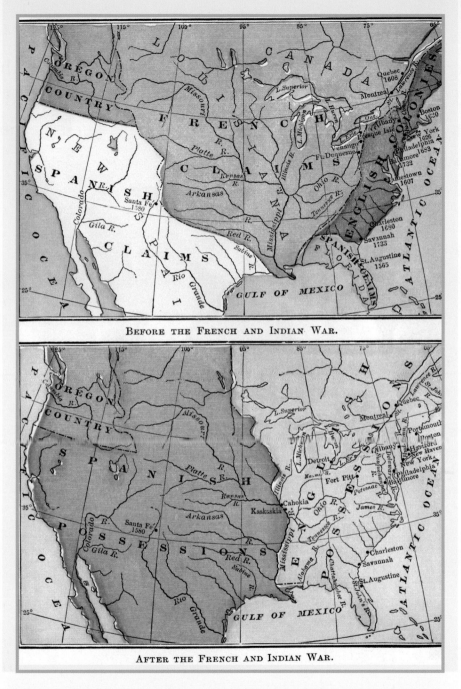

BEFORE THE FRENCH AND INDIAN WAR.

AFTER THE FRENCH AND INDIAN WAR.

These maps show the European countries that owned North America before and after the French and Indian War. The English gains are shown in green on the bottom map.

and signatures were written on pieces of fine leather vellum that would last for centuries to come. Years of struggle and change still lay ahead, but hardworking Americans such as the tanner would help the new nation thrive.

Glossary

apprentice	a person who works with an expert to learn a new skill or job
barter	to exchange goods or services rather than money
bate	a mixture of animal dung, salt, and water used to clean lime from a skin
boycott	to stop buying a product or using a service as a form of protest
craftsmen	trained workers who make objects by hand
cure	to preserve a material so it does not rot
currying	the process of making leather soft and flexible
felt	a material used to make hats
imported	bought from other regions or countries
indenture	a contract requiring a person to serve an employer as a worker or apprentice for a specific amount of time
journeyman	a craftsman who has completed his apprenticeship
leather	cured, hairless animal skin
lime	a calcium compound that is made by crushing and melting seashells
livestock	farm animals that are raised to produce food
mill	a machine used to grind something
ooze	a liquid containing bark and water
steers	young male cows
tan	to turn an animal skin into leather
tannins	yellowish-brown chemicals found in plants
tanyard	a tanner's facility, including buildings and outdoor spaces where tanning takes place
vellum	a paperlike material made from very thin sheets of leather

Find Out More

BOOKS

Kalman, Bobbie. *A Visual Dictionary of a Colonial Community.* New York: Crabtree Publishing Company, 2008.

Love, Rebecca. *English Colonies in America.* Mankato, MN: Compass Point Books, 2008.

Thompson, Linda. *The First Settlements.* Vero Beach, FL: Rourke Publishing, 2006.

Winter, Kay, and Larry Day. *Colonial Voices: Hear Them Speak.* New York: Dutton Juvenile, 2008.

WEBSITES

Boot and Shoemaker

www.history.org/Almanack/life/trades/tradesho.cfm
Learn more about the work of shoemakers who lived in Colonial Williamsburg, and take a peek inside the shoemaker's shop that is open to visitors in that historic village.

Colonial House

www.pbs.org/wnet/colonialhouse/history/index.html
This page, associated with PBS's television series *Colonial House,* offers interactive features.

Colonial Williamsburg Kids Zone

www.history.org/kids/

Tour the colonial capital of Virginia and meet some of its important residents.
There are games, activities, and many resources about colonial life and history.

Jump Back in Time: Colonial America (from the Library of Congress)

www.americaslibrary.gov/jb/colonial/jb_colonial_subj.html

Read about the history of colonial America.

Index

Page numbers in **boldface** are illustrations.

About the Author

Christine Petersen has enjoyed diverse careers as a bat biologist and middle school teacher. Now a freelance writer, she has published more than forty nonfiction books for children and young adults. Her most recent books for Marshall Cavendish are *The Apothecary*, *The Blacksmith*, and *The Surveyor*, in this series. In her free time, Petersen conducts naturalist programs near her Minnesota home and spends time with her young son. She is a member of the Society of Children's Book Writers and Illustrators.